Copyright Notice

The material enclosed is copyrighted. You do not have resell rights or giveaway rights to the material provided herein. Only customers that have purchased this material are authorized to view it. If you think you may have an illegally distributed copy of this material, please contact us immediately.

No part of this publication may be reproduced or transmitted in any form or by any means, electronic or mechanical, including photocopying or by information storage and retrieval systems. It is illegal to copy this material and publish it on another web site, news group, forum, etc. even if you include the copyright notice.

Legal Notice

While all attempts have been made to verify information provided in this publication, neither the author nor the publisher assumes any responsibility for errors, omissions or contrary interpretation of the subject matter herein. The publisher wants to stress that the information contained herein may be subject to varying state and/or local laws or regulations. All users are advised to retain competent counsel to determine what state and/or local laws or regulations may apply to the user's particular operation. The purchaser or reader of this publication assumes responsibility for the use of these materials and information. Adherence to all applicable laws and regulations, federal, state and local, governing professional licensing, operation practices, and all other aspects of operation in the US or any other jurisdiction is the sole responsibility of the purchaser or reader. The publisher and author assume no responsibility or liability whatsoever on the behalf of any purchaser or reader of these materials. Any perceived slights of specific people or organizations is unintentional.

INTRODUCTION

25 FUN AND EASY SCIENCE EXPERIMENTS THAT SHOW THE NATURE OF GOD

Inside every child is a natural scientist. Kids love to examine God's creation with their hands - often far more than they love to read and write about it! If there is a mystery in the way water behaves in straws or under heat lamps, they want to know the whys and hows. If light creates a rainbow on the wall, they demand an explanation.

Our science experiments take very little time and fit any budget. Also, they require only items found in every household, except for a few that can easily be purchased at the local hardware store.

Another fun thing about our science experiments is that they demonstrate God and his nature every time. God may seem a bit mysterious to kids because he's supposed to love us even more than parents, yet he can't be seen and heard like parents. He doesn't hug, kiss goodnight, or help pick up toys. Science ought to be seen as a joyful means of discovering the nature of God, and each of our experiments attempts to show either a parallel to him or an insight into his character.

Each experiment contains a **Scripture Verse** and an **Understanding God** section to accompany a **List of Materials,** set of **Steps,** an **Answer** to a question the experiment raises, and an **Explanation** of why the answer is correct in scientific terms.

This set of experiments is divided into five groups, those dealing with **Light, Color, Motion, Magnetism,** and **Gravity,** as these are some of the essential basics of God's creation. You will find the instructions easy to follow, the materials easy to find, and the mess easy to clean up - if there's any mess at all.

Hopefully your students will also find that science is fun, easy, and not at all intimidating! And also, they'll know enough about the nature of God to find him as real as the materials involved - the very ones he created!

Contents

Introduction 3

Five Experiments Using Light 5
Experiment #1: Water and Light & Optical Illusions 6
Experiment #2: Making Water Stand U 8
Experiment #3: Using Water as a Magnifier 10
Experiment #4: Understanding Shadows 12
Experiment #5: Defining Light and Dark Through Shadow People 14

Five Experiments Using Color 16
Experiment #1: Using a Color Wheel 17
Experiment #2: Understanding How Rainbows are Made 19
Experiment #3: Separating Colors 21
Experiment #4: Using Bubbles to See Colors 23
Experiment #5: Using Dye to Dilute Color 25

Five Experiments Using Motion 27
Experiment #1: Demonstrating and Breaking "Inertia" 28
Experiment #2: Harnessing the Power of Air to Move Things 30
Experiment #3: Spinning Buttons to Understand the Importance of Good Behavior 32
Experiment #4: Using the Wind's Motion to Understand God's Will 34
Experiment #5: Coins in Motion Show God's Protection 36

Five Experiments Using Magnetism 38
Experiment #1: How One Magnet Creates Another Magnet 39
Experiment #2: A "maze" ing Magnets 41
Experiment #3: Can a Magnet Rescue a Drowning Paper Clip? 43
Experiment #4: Creating an Electromagnet 45
Experiment #5: Showing How Opposites Attract in Magnets 47

Five Experiments Using Gravity 49
Experiment #1: Gravity Doesn't Care About Weight 50
Experiment #2: Finding the Center of Gravity to Create Balance 52
Experiment #3: Changing the Center of Gravity Keeps the Disciple Standing 54
Experiment #4: How Heat Affects Gravity 56
Experiment #5: Putting a Spin on Gravity 58

Five Experiments Using Light

Light is a form of energy. It travels in rays, and the reason you see objects, regardless of their color, is that light reflects off of them. When Jesus said in John 8:12, "I am the light of the world," he was expressing a great truth. We can only see the path to God because he shines the way. In this section, we'll get to see many likenesses between the light in our world and the Light of the World.

EXPERIMENT #1

WATER AND LIGHT & OPTICAL ILLUSIONS

RELATED SCRIPTURE:

Matthew 19:30 But many who are the greatest now will be least important then, and those who seem least important now will be the greatest then.

MATERIALS:

- Eight crayons, different colors
- One clear drinking glass with a wide mouth
- Tap water

STEPS:

1. Arrange the crayons with the tips pointed down in the empty glass and their middles resting on the side of the glass
2. Spread them out evenly so there is equal space between them

Do the crayons look straight or bent through the glass?

3. Slowly, pour tap water into the glass, keeping the crayons still
4. Stop when the glass is half full so the crayons don't float off

Do the crayons look straight or bent through the water?

ANSWER:

Before adding water, the crayons will look straight as they rest in the glass. After adding water, they will look bent at the water line.

EXPLANATION:

Light travels through both air and water in rays. The speed of light is very swift—so swift you could never follow it with your eye. However it slows down in water. The slowing makes the rays change direction slightly, and that's what gives the crayons the look of being bent. It is what we call an "optical illusion," something that looks different from what it actually is.

UNDERSTANDING GOD:

God is very anxious to show us that in this world, things are often not as they appear. What works with crayons and water is also true with friendships and groups of people. Some people like to be admired for their clothes, possessions, and looks. But often the very best people are those we'd never notice from what's on the outside. Don't fall for the optical illusion of popularity. Jesus said about the kingdom of heaven in Matthew 19:30, "Many who are the greatest now will be least important then, and those who seem least important now will be the greatest then." Instead of looking to be admired, look to serve others and be nice. You'll be a whole lot more prepared for all eternity with Jesus if you "see things straight" down here.

EXPERIMENT #2

MAKING WATER STAND UP

RELATED SCRIPTURE:

Exodus 14:21 And Moses stretched out his hand over the sea; and the Lord caused the sea to go back by a strong east wind all that night, and made the sea dry land, and the waters were divided.

MATERIALS:

- Drinking straw
- Glass
- Tap water

STEPS:

1. Fill the drinking glass with water
2. Stick the straw straight down into the water so that the straw is filled up to the water line
3. Put your thumb over the top of the straw, completely covering it
4. Pull the straw straight up out of the water

What happens to the water in the straw?

ANSWER:

The water defies the force of gravity and remains inside the straw.

EXPLANATION:

When liquid enters a straw, some air must leave the straw. This makes for less air pressure inside the straw. When you put your thumb over the top of the straw and lift it, the air pressure outside the straw is greater than the air pressure inside. The water is held in place because there is not enough air pressure to force it back down. When you release your thumb from the straw, you allow air to flow back into through the top, and the water drops out the bottom.

UNDERSTANDING GOD:

Just as water can stand in a straw, it can also move at the command of God. Experiments like this should remind us that all things are possible, and with every scientific rule we think we know, there is one lurking that can make that first rule null and void. This can help us understand how God parted the Red Sea. Some folks say it was done by strong winds; others say it was done by strong tides; some say it didn't happen at all and is just a big myth. When we hear someone doubt God's miracles, we should remember the water standing up in the straw. God can do anything with water that he feels like - including parting the Red Sea, turning water into wine, and having Jesus walk on its surface!

EXPERIMENT #3

USING WATER AS A MAGNIFIER

RELATED SCRIPTURE:

Colossians 3:1-2 "If ye then be risen with Christ, seek those things which are above…set your affections on things above, not on things of the earth."

MATERIALS:

- Clear Glass
- Tap water
- Two pennies

STEPS:

1. Drop the pennies beside one another on the floor
2. Fill your glass with tap water
3. Put it on top of one penny and let the water settle
4. Stand up and then compare the two

Which penny looks bigger? Which looks closer?

ANSWER:

The penny under the glass, to some people, looks like it's somehow been raised maybe an inch off the floor. To others, it merely looks slightly bigger.

EXPLANATION:

As light enters the water in the glass, the speed at which it is traveling slows down. The rounded shape of the glass (and hence, of the water) causes the light to bend outwards. As it bends, it extends the image it surrounds outward slightly as well, making the object appear larger. It works as a magnifier. This is one reason never to trust what you see when jumping into a pool or lake. The bottom of the water can look closer than it is, and people jumped in water over their heads, thinking they would be able to stand up easily.

UNDERSTANDING GOD:

This experiment shows us again that things are not always as they appear. Things were made to look bigger than they actually were. In this life, we make a big deal out of things like cars and houses and clothes and possessions. They take up a big space in our minds—sometimes too often! But Colossians 3:1 tells us, "If ye then be risen with Christ, seek those things which are above…set your affections on things above, not on things of the earth." When we get to heaven, the glass will be taken away. We'll see then how small and unimportant those things really were. Love the Lord your God with all your heart, soul and strength, and love your neighbor as yourself. Then, God will give you just the right amount of all that good stuff.

Experiment #4

Understanding Shadows

Related Scripture:

Psalm 23:4 Yea though I walk through the valley of the Shadow of Death, I will fear no evil.

Materials:

- Flashlight
- Wall

Steps:

1. In the off position, put the mouth of a flashlight flush against a wall
2. Turn the flashlight on.
3. Pull the flashlight slowly back from the wall

What happens to the beam of the light?

4. Put your finger in the beam between the flashlight and the wall
5. Move the flashlight back farther

What happens to the reflection of your finger?

Answer:

As you take the flashlight farther from the wall, the beam should get bigger but also less intense. If you hold your finger steady, its shadow should also get bigger as the light moves further away.

Explanation:

A beam of light grows, rather than getting smaller, when you move the light source further away. This has to do with the direction of the beams. In a flashlight, the face is round and the rim is very shallow, maybe half an inch deep at most. This allows the light to move forward in a beam (as opposed to a light bulb, which will send light in all directions). However, the shallowness of the rim allows the beam to spread out, so that

when it hits the wall, it is bigger than the actual source and will continue to grow bigger as more space is put between the light and the wall.

To create a shadow, you need three things: A light, a solid object, and a surface. A shadow will always fall opposite the light source that creates it. Light will shine through some surfaces such as fabric, but it will not shine through solid objects like your finger. The shadow size will depend on the distance between the light, the object, and its source. If the object (finger) is brought closer to the light and away from the source, its shadow grows smaller and crisper. If it is brought farther from the light and closer to the source, it grows bigger, though the edges are less crisp.

UNDERSTANDING GOD:

Shadows can be fun to play with, but they represent an absence of light. This world can be a shadow place sometimes and seem scary. Bullies lurk, illnesses threaten, family members argue, and fears of things that could happen keep us awake at night. We need to remember that God is like that flashlight; he never ceases to shine, no matter how many shadows pass between us and him. And often, the things we fear turn out to be nothing more than shadows! If we pass through a shadowy time in life—like our own "valley of the shadow of death" mentioned in Psalm 23, we need to remember that God's love and light will never cease to shine upon us.

EXPERIMENT #5

DEFINING LIGHT AND DARK THROUGH SHADOW PEOPLE

RELATED SCRIPTURE:

Psalm 119:105 Thy word is a lamp unto my feet, and a light unto my path.

MATERIALS:

- Lamp without a shade
- Table
- Chair
- Piece of poster board or a large piece of paper
- Masking tape
- Pencil or marker

STEPS:

1. Turn the lamp on, and place it on a table two feet away from a wall
2. Have a friend sit in a chair so that his head is between the light bulb and the wall
3. Tape the poster board on the wall so that it captures your friend's whole head
4. Trace around the image of his head on the paper. Go slowly and carefully

How closely does the shape you drew resemble your friend's actual profile?

ANSWERS:

If you went slowly, the image you created should bear a great resemblance to your friend's profile!

EXPLANATION:

Two things go into the clarity of the image on the wall. The first is the short distance between the light and the wall. Shorter distances create crisper, more realistic shadows. The second thing is the strength and size of the light bulb. Even a 40-watt bulb would throw enough light to create a crisp shadow at two feet. If we tried this with a small light from a flashlight, the beam would not be wide enough, and the light might not be strong enough to create a clean image all around.

UNDERSTANDING GOD:

While the ways of God are often very mysterious to us, he leaves us 'outlines' so that we can 'trace out' his nature and see him more clearly. The Bible sheds great light on God. We can read Bible stories and get an understanding of what he is like. Studying God's word helps us to create an image of God's nature, which we can then use to make decisions that will please him most. As the Psalmist says, "Thy word is a lamp unto my feet and a light unto my path!"

Five Experiments Using Color

God could have created for us a gray, drab, colorless world. But color in and of itself reveals some things about him. Some days *are* drab and gray, which is like our time on earth. When the sun comes out and everything glimmers and is colorful, it reminds us of God's promise that someday we will live in the ultimately beautiful, colorful heaven with him. God wants us to know that he is the ultimate artist, and when we experiment with his colors, he is happy that we are exploring his creation. So let's do some experiments with color that will show us more and more about his nature.

EXPERIMENT #1

USING A COLOR WHEEL

RELATED SCRIPTURE:

1 Timothy 3:16: Great indeed, we confess, is the mystery of godliness: He was manifested in the flesh, vindicated by the Spirit..

MATERIALS:

- Glass or cup without too-wide a lip (juice glass or small paper cup works best)
- Half-sheets of paper
- Scissors
- Pencils
- One red marker, one blue marker (crayons may substitute)

STEPS:

1. Put the glass over the sheet of paper and trace a perfect circle
2. Cut out the circle
3. Divide the circle into four equal triangles by drawing an "X" across it, with the lines meeting in the middle
4. Cut two TINY slits, using the two lines of the "X," for the pencil to poke through
5. Color two of the four triangular sections—one red, one blue—so that the colored triangles are opposite each other. Leave the other two sections white.
6. Poke the pencil through from top to bottom so that the point is facing downward
7. Spin the pencil so that the color wheel spins like a top.

What happens to the red, white and blue?

ANSWER:

The colors should blend together. If your students are good spinners, they should see something akin to pastel purple.

EXPLANATION:

When mixed together, colors change. Many colors, when mixed together, will make some dull shade of brown. However, red and blue are two colors which, when combined, create another brilliant color—purple. The additional white should lighten it up, the result being a pastel purple.

UNDERSTANDING GOD:

A color wheel is a good way to understand a difficult concept: The Holy Trinity. The trinity has three members, Father, Son, and Holy Spirit, who are separate, yet are one. It sounds like a contradiction! But when we spin our color wheel, we can use it as a symbol. Christ is symbolized by the red for his blood; the Holy Spirit is symbolized by blue, as he is often associated with water; the Father is the purity of white.

In motion, which they always are because God never sleeps (Psalm 121:4), they act as one complete circle of love—three in one! When Jesus confessed, "I and the Father are one" in John 10:30, people didn't know what to make of it. They asked, "How could God be up there where we can pray to him and also down here as you?" The color wheel helps us to understand that. 1 Timothy 3:16 defines the Trinity as manifest or revealed in Jesus and believed through the Holy Spirit. They spin into our lives together!

EXPERIMENT #2

UNDERSTANDING HOW RAINBOWS ARE MADE

RELATED SCRIPTURE:

Genesis 9:13

I have set my **rainbow** in the clouds, and it will be the sign of the covenant between me and the earth.

MATERIALS:

- Table or floor space with exposure to sunlight
- Pan without deep sides, such as a frying pan
- Tap water
- Vegetable oil
- Eyedropper

STEPS:

1. Fill the pan with water almost to the top.
2. While not putting it directly in the sun, put the pan near a spot that is in the sun's direct path.
3. Have children move their heads slowly around the sides of the pan until they reach the angle where the sun is beaming at them.
4. Have them stop right there, observing the water.
5. Put an eyedropper of vegetable oil into the pan
6. Have them observe the colors that appear, moving toward the far side of the pan
7. Have them blow on the water next.

What happened when you added the oil? What happened when you blew on the drop of oil?

ANSWER:

The added oil should have made a rainbow appear moving toward the outside of the pan.

Blowing on the oil should have made the rainbow swirl and bend.

TeachSundaySchool.com

EXPLANATION:

It is often said that oil and water don't mix, which is true. But they work well together. Water will absorb the sun's rays, but it won't separate them for us if we are merely staring into the water. Oil absorbs and then refracts, or separates, and hence we can begin to see the colors. When blowing on the oil, the light rays have to bend, and this creates more color with more movement.

UNDERSTANDING GOD:

In Genesis 9:13 God showed a rainbow as a symbol to Noah after the Great Flood. The rainbow symbolized his promise that he would always be with mankind. When we see rainbows, we can let them serve as one of God's reminders that he is with us, no matter what "storms" are going on in our lives.

In this experiment, it's sort of like we're the water, God is the oil. When we put the two together, we see a rainbow, which is a symbol of God's love and presence. Without God, we're just clear and shallow and boring. With just one drop of God, we're colorful and dimensional—and fun to play with.

Experiment #3

Separating Colors

Related Scripture:

2 Corinthians 5:17 Therefore if any man be in Christ, he is a new creature: old things are passed away; behold, all things are become new.

Materials:

- One clear glass
- Tap water
- One sheet of white paper
- A windowsill with direct sunlight (This won't work on a cloudy day!)

Steps:

1. Fill the glass with water so it is nearly full
2. Place it on a windowsill
3. Put a piece of white paper onto the floor
4. Move it around until it picks up color that has been shed by the glass. This will not be in the direct path of sunlight but off to the side. Where, exactly, depends on the size of the glass and the amount of water. Be patient in your pursuit of the colors.

What do you see?

Answer:

You should see a rainbow.

Explanation:

When the sun shines *through* water and comes out on the other side, the water will have separated out the colors that make up white light or sunlight. When light passes through water, the water's density will make those colors change direction. What we're seeing is "refracted," or separated, light. Each color that makes up white light responds differently to water. Purple bends the most, and red bends the least. The result is the colors sorted out on the paper. Light bends when it passes through water, which explains why the rainbow is not in the exact line of the sun beaming through the glass off to the side.

UNDERSTANDING GOD:

The most difficult part of this experiment may have been finding your rainbow on the floor. Rainbows are signs of God's presence in our hearts and our lives (Genesis 9:13). The Apostle Paul assures us in 2 Corinthians 5:17 that we are new creatures when we accept Christ into our hearts and that God will always be with us to lead, guide, love, encourage, and protect. However, sometimes it seems hard to find God's presence. Sometimes it's hard to figure out what he's saying to us or doing in our lives. However, just like the sun and the glass and the water, God is *always* there. To find his will and see him clearly, sometimes we need patience. We need to be at the right "angle"; we have to be behaving in his will to receive his most colorful promises and messages.

Experiment #4

Using Bubbles to See Colors

Related Scripture:

Hebrews 7:25: Consequently, [Jesus] is able to save to the uttermost *all* those who draw near to God through him, since he always lives to make intercession for them.

Materials:

- Standard-size bottle of bubbles with bubble-blowing stick
- Sugar, one teaspoon
- Direct sunlight

Steps:

1. Put a teaspoon of sugar into the bubbles (which will prevent bubbles from popping as easily)
2. Put the cap back on and shake it up
3. Put the bottle in the refrigerator for half an hour (so the bubble liquid can settle again)
4. Bring the bottle over to the sunlight and sit down on the floor, placing the bottle in front of you
5. Blow a good-size bubble through the ring at the end of the blowing stick. Try not to blow so hard that the bubble dislodges from the ring
6. Once you have a good-size bubble attached to the ring, sit the blower stick gently on top of the bottle of bubbles, using its mouth as a stand
7. Observe the bubble

What do you see? How does the bubble change over time?

8. Repeat the experiment three or four times

How are the bubbles different from one another?

ANSWERS:

You should notice that after a few moments, colors of the rainbow begin to appear on the bubble. The colors should change, move, and eventually disappear. You will notice that every bubble responds slightly differently from the ones preceding it. The colors may show up more slowly or quickly. They will have a different pattern and will last for different durations before disappearing again.

EXPLANATION:

At first, the light will pass through the bubble. However, the air inside the bubble soon changes. The carbon dioxide blown into it begins to dissipate. Some of the white light or sunlight is not able to pass through, and it will separate, or "refract," on the bubble's inner and outer lining. Actually made of fluid, the lining of the bubble is constantly changing thickness. That's why the colors move and eventually disappear.

As you observe other bubbles, you will notice that each one reacts to light a little differently. This has to do with the bubble's thickness and hence its response to gravity, which will pull the liquid slowly downward, making each bubble thinner at the top. How much light is refracted depends on how thick the bubble was to begin with and how long it remains on the stand.

UNDERSTANDING GOD:

Bubbles seem like one of the simplest of God's creations. It's amazing to see how each bubble is a little different from the others in how it refracts light. God works like this in our lives. We're all different, so he is likely to show up differently in all of us. He may give one person the gift of kindness. Another person may seem less friendly but is very good with mathematics. Another is shy with people but loves animals. We're all simply people—God's creation—but as attested to in Hebrews 7:25, there are not two of us alike, and God is able to save us all and shine his light uniquely through each of us!

EXPERIMENT #5

USING DYE TO DILUTE COLOR
(DILUTE MEANS "MAKE WEAKER")

RELATED SCRIPTURE:

2 Corinthians 6:14: Do not be yoked together with unbelievers. For what do righteousness and wickedness have in common? Or what fellowship can light have with darkness?

MATERIALS:

- Two squares of white fabric, 2-inches-by-2 inches (cut up an old t-shirt or towel)
- Two small plastic cups
- Tap water
- Red food coloring

STEPS:

1. Fill one cup almost to the top with water
2. Fill the other cup with water only about 1/8 of an inch
3. Drop two drops of the red food coloring into each
4. Swirl the cups gently until the food coloring dissolves
5. Pour several drops from the full cup onto the t-shirt square
6. Pour several drops from the other cup onto the other t-shirt square

What do you notice that the two drops of food coloring did in different amounts of water? How do they differ when spilled onto the fabric?

ANSWER:

The colored water from the fuller glass will be a dull pinkish color and will not change the color of the fabric very much. The colored water from the emptier glass will be redder in the glass and more vibrant on the fabric.

EXPLANATION:

Food coloring works like a dye. The more water you add, the lighter the color you are creating. You are actually dyeing the fabric by pouring the colored water onto it. Water

dilutes, or makes other liquids weaker. This is why, when you make really sour lemonade, your mom might cringe at the strong lemon flavor and say, "Add some water!" We may not like strong lemonade, but we all like strong colors. If we want vibrant colors, we know to add less water to the coloring agent.

Understanding God:

This experiment symbolizes what God says in the Bible about picking our friends carefully. In 2 Corinthians 6:14, the Apostle Paul says it like this: "Don't be yoked together with nonbelievers." Sometimes we pick friends who don't love God and aren't trying to do good. They can be fun, but can weaken our faith by either distracting us from our daily thoughts about God or by actually tempting us to get into trouble.

They are like the full glass of water. We may be strong before we "mix up" with them, but after they've been around us for a while, our faith is dull and our love of Christ barely shows.

We want to pick friends who will help us keep our faith vibrant. They won't water us down, and others will still be able to see Christ's "colorful" presence strongly in our lives. These friends are like the glass without much diluted water.

Be friendly to all, but pick your best friends carefully if you want to remain spiritually colorful!

Five Experiments Using Motion

Many Christians wonder how to know the will of God in their lives. One wise man suggested, "It is easier to turn a moving ship than a still ship." He meant that if you keep moving and try out various choices, God will "turn you" and get you moving in the right direction. He'll close a door if it's not the right one and give you signs along the way. Such is better than trying to figure out God's will by doing nothing—simply sitting still.

By trying experiments with motion, we can demonstrate lots about finding God's will in our lives. So let's do some experiments that will show us just that.

EXPERIMENT #1

DEMONSTRATING AND BREAKING "INERTIA"

RELATED SCRIPTURE:

Isaiah 40:29 He gives strength to the weary and increases the power of the weak.

MATERIALS:

- Hardback book (kind of heavy)
- Piece of string, three times as long as the length of the book
- Rubber band

STEPS:

1. Tie the string around the book lengthwise and make a knot
2. Use the string that dangles from the knot as a tail and tie a rubber band to the tail using another double knot
3. Dangle the book by rubber band attached to the string for a moment, just to test the strength of your knots. They should not come apart under that much pressure.
4. Lay the book on a scratchy rug or large carpet
5. Using the rubber band, give the book a few tugs.

What happens with each tug? Do you have to pull harder on the rubber band, less hard, or about the same as the first tug?

ANSWER:

The first time, you should have to tug a lot harder than the second and third and fourth times.

EXPLANATION:

This demonstrates the principle of inertia as defined by Sir Isaac Newton (who also discovered gravity). Inertia means "not moving," and the principle of inertia is that things not moving will remain still until another force comes along and starts it moving again.

At first, the book was in a state of inertia. After tugging once, the state was broken, and hence you should not have had to pull the rubber band as hard after the first try.

UNDERSTANDING GOD:

Oftentimes we become like that book. We are not moving forward in our lives. We're not meeting new people, learning new things, or even acting curious about understanding God or his world around us. When inertia sets in, we become couch potatoes who would rather vegetate in front of the lives of others (watch mindless TV shows) or play video games. The longer we do this, the harder it is for us to get out of our state of inertia.

The Holy Spirit is like that string—always wrapped around us—trying to urge us toward youth group or Sunday school or to work for that charity on Saturday instead of sitting home. At first we often think, "No way; I'd rather stay home." But if we try it, we're often glad we came!

Don't let inertia keep you from reaching out to others—or from experiencing God's world the way he wants you to! According to Isaiah 40:29, he brings strength to the weary—even those of who have no strength—those deep in inertia!

EXPERIMENT #2

HARNESSING THE POWER OF AIR TO MOVE THINGS

RELATED SCRIPTURE:

Philippians 4:13: I can do all things in him who strengthens me.

MATERIALS:

- Two chairs
- Piece of twine, five feet long
- Drinking straw
- Scissors
- Scotch tape
- Large balloon (as opposed to a water balloon)

STEPS:

1. Cut a five-inch piece of straw, cutting off the accordion part that allows it to bend. The five-inch piece should be completely straight
2. Loop it through the string
3. Tie the ends of the string around the two chairs
4. Pull the chairs apart so the string is tight and the straw is straight.
5. Blow up the balloon and keep the end pinched
6. Have another person lay two or three pieces of tape across the straw and bring the balloon underneath of it, so that the balloon is now taped to the straw. The pinched end of the balloon should be facing one of the chairs.
7. Let the balloon go

What happens to the straw when you let go of the balloon?

ANSWER:

It should move along the string closer to the chair facing away from the balloon opening.

EXPLANATION:

This is an interesting way of seeing forward motion that doesn't involve wheels. Most things that we set in motion in our culture, such as cars, motorcycles, and trains, use wheels to perpetuate momentum. However, some things need only air.

When we blew into the balloon, we created pressure, or we "harnessed" the air for a useful purpose. When we let go of the balloon, it emptied itself to relieve the pressure, and the straw moved along the string. Straws are very light. A heavier object requires more air pressure.

One complicated use of air pressure involves rocket launches to start space travel. Enough air pressure can lift a very heavy rocket off the ground and help set it into orbit.

UNDERSTANDING GOD:

Without the Holy Spirit in our lives, we are very much like that straw. We may look busy, but without God's direction, our lives are all but meaningless. Once we give our lives to God, it's as if he harnesses a great spiritual energy source to us. The balloon is like the Holy Spirit. Without all that power, we would never be able to get where we're going! Just like a plain old straw can move with the help of harnessed air, we can do all things through Christ who strengthens us! (Philippians 4:13)

EXPERIMENT #3

SPINNING BUTTONS TO UNDERSTAND THE IMPORTANCE OF GOOD BEHAVIOR

RELATED SCRIPTURE:

Proverbs 3:6 In all your ways acknowledge Him, and He will make your paths straight

MATERIALS:

- String
- Scissors
- Button with two holes large enough to thread the string through

STEPS:

1. Cut a length of string a foot long
2. Thread the button onto the string
3. Hold one end of the string in each hand with the button sagging slightly in the middle
4. Using circular motions, with both hands circling toward you, let the button circle a dozen or so times. This will twist the string
5. Pull tightly on both ends of the string

What happens to the button?

ANSWER:

The button should spin rapidly until the thread is completely unraveled.

EXPLANATION:

This experiment shows the principle of harnessing energy. When we twisted the string, we transferred energy to the string. That is like "stored energy" that hasn't been used yet. Stored energy is sometimes used in complex utilities such as windmills and waterwheels. Water or wind is often contained and pressurized so that it will be very powerful when it is used.

When you tighten the string, you are un-harnessing the stored energy or putting it in a state of "kinesis" or movement. Once released, it causes the button to spin until the energy is spent.

UNDERSTANDING GOD:

Just like energy, God is always with us, but when he's moving in our lives—that's when we are the liveliest! Oftentimes our lives "slouch" like the string. We're not on the straight and narrow, and may even be doing crooked things! We need to "straighten out" before we can use God's good energy. Once we're on the straight and narrow again, our lives start to spin and move in such dynamic ways that it will attract the attention of others. Proverbs 3:6 says, "In *all* your ways, acknowledge or include God, and He will make your paths *straight!*"

Experiment #4

Using the Wind's Motion to Understand God's Will

Related Scripture:

John 3:8: The wind blows where it wishes and you hear the sound of it, but do not know where it comes from and where it is going; so is everyone who is born of the Spirit.

Materials:

- A calm day (not very windy)
- Your finger
- Water

Steps:

1. Go outside
2. Stand in a place where you will not be protected from the wind
3. Either wet your finger with water from a bottle or simply stick your finger in your mouth up to your knuckle and get it wet on all sides
4. Stick your finger into the air

What happens to your finger?

Answer:

Even if you can't feel any wind, you should start to feel cold on one side of your finger—from the direction the slightest breeze is blowing from.

Explanation:

Motion can speed up evaporation, the process of liquid turning to gas. The motion of the wind caused the spit or water on one side of your finger to evaporate more rapidly than what was on the other side. The evaporation will provide a cold sensation. You can know which way the wind is blowing by determining which side of your finger turns cold first.

UNDERSTANDING GOD:

In John 3:8, Jesus compared the presence of God in a believer's life to hearing the wind: "The wind blows where it wishes and you hear the sound of it, but do not know where it comes from and where it is going; so is everyone who is born of the Spirit." As Christians we have the great and wonderful gift of being able to sense, feel, and even spiritually "hear" God in our lives. That doesn't mean we understand him all the time. Just like we can't see the wind, we can't always see where God is taking us. We can learn the direction of the wind by sticking a wet finger into the air and feeling deep down where the cold is. We can get understanding from God by feeling deep down in prayer and seeking his direction. It's all a bit mysterious, but God wants us to seek him daily.

EXPERIMENT #5

COINS IN MOTION SHOW GOD'S PROTECTION

RELATED SCRIPTURE:

Psalm 37:24 Though he fall, he shall not be utterly cast down: for the Lord upholds him with His hand.

MATERIALS:

- One quarter for each student

STEPS:

Have students

1. Put their elbows out in front of them so that the part of their arm from the elbow to the wrist is parallel to the floor
2. Turn their wrists so their palms are facing up
3. Place a quarter about a inch from their elbows on the top, flat part of their arms
4. Drop their arms very quickly with an open hand

Did you catch the quarter? *Almost?* **Try it again!**

ANSWER:

After a few tries, most students can catch the quarter so easily that they are amazed. It's as if the quarter "wanders" into their hands if they drop their arms fast enough.

EXPLANATION:

We're back to the principle of inertia that we illustrated in Experiment #1 of Motion. The quarter is in a state of inertia when you start out. The force of gravity will definitely pull it downward once you drop your elbow, but the fall is slow getting started due to inertia. Your arm, however, is already in motion, moving rapidly as you drop your elbow quickly. Hence it has time to catch the quarter before inertia gives way to the gravitational pull.

UNDERSTANDING GOD:

Have you ever been in such a big jam that you thought not even God could get you out of it? God often lets us suffer the consequences of our actions and even the best of people will have their faith tested. You can sometimes feel a lot like that quarter—like you're going to hit the ground and die due to some scary circumstance in your life. But Psalm 37:24 says that though men frequently fall a ways, man will not be utterly cast down—will not hit the ground with a splatter! Why? Because the Lord upholds us in his hand. No matter what our scary problem is or how much like falling it feels, God is swift enough and strong enough to catch us!

Five Experiments Using Magnetism

Magnetism causes a lot of behavior on planet earth that we might not expect. A small, simple horseshoe magnet can move a sewing needle without touching it. It can cause things heavier than water to rise through water. It can make things fly through the air. God has magnetism also, and he causes people to do extraordinary things that would seem impossible. Let's use experiments in magnetism to help get us into God's "magnetic field" and become the super creatures we were designed to be.

EXPERIMENT #1

HOW ONE MAGNET CREATES ANOTHER MAGNET

RELATED SCRIPTURE:

James 4:8 Draw near to God, and He will draw near to you.

MATERIALS:

- One-inch horseshoe magnet
- Sewing needle

STEPS:

1. Hold the sewing needle up to the magnet
2. Let go

Does the sewing needle stick to the magnet?

3. Pinch the sewing needle between your thumb and finger at the halfway point
4. Take the magnet and, using one end of the horseshoe only, rub the needle from your finger out to the point.
5. Stroke the needle 50 times this way with the magnet, going always in the same direction, always using the same end of the magnet
6. Turn the needle and the magnet around.
7. Using the other end of the horseshoe only, rub the needle from your finger out to the eye
8. Stroke the needle 50 times this way with the magnet, going always in the same direction, always using the same end of the magnet
9. Put the needle on the table. Hold the magnet right over top of it.

Does the sewing needle stick to the magnet?

ANSWER:

Before rubbing the magnet against the needle, it would not stick. After rubbing the needle, it should stick.

EXPLANATION:

Essentially we have created a magnet out of a nonmagnetic needle. By rubbing the magnet's north and south poles against the two ends of the needle, we gave it magnetic pull. While this only works on ionized metals (not coins, copper or scrap), repeated friction with a magnet caused the atoms inside the needle to rearrange themselves. Magnets are formed when all the atoms inside an object line up in a certain order. The friction drew them into order, and a new magnet was created.

UNDERSTANDING GOD:

When we accept Jesus into our hearts, we are said to be new creations. Part of that is that we are "magnetized" to God by drawing him close to us. While before, we might have felt spiritually limp or unmoving, now we can draw near to God and be pulled in the directions he wants us to go! As the saying goes from James 4:8, draw near to God, and then he will draw near to you!

EXPERIMENT #2

A "MAZE"ING MAGNETS

RELATED SCRIPTURE:

Proverbs 3:5-6 Trust in the Lord with all your heart and lean not unto your own understanding; in all your ways acknowledge Him, and He will make your paths straight

MATERIALS

- Piece of cardboard at least one-foot by six-inches
- Marker pen
- One-inch horseshoe magnet
- Paper clip

STEPS

1. Draw a maze on the piece of cardboard
2. Hold the cardboard out in front of you
3. Place a paper clip at the start
4. Hold the magnet underneath the cardboard just under the paper clip
5. Try to move the paper clip through the maze just by using the magnet

Did the paper clip get lost or stuck in the maze?

ANSWER:

The magnet should be able to move the paper clip along the maze and out to the end if you have patience and persistence.

EXPLANATION:

Magnets can create other magnets from certain metals. But the magnetic field will pass through most other substances, and its strength on the other side depends on the substance's width and its resistance to magnetization. Cardboard is relatively thin— thin enough for the magnetic field to pass through—and its resistance to magnetization is weak. Hence the magnetic field on the other side of the cardboard will still be very strong, and the magnet will be able to push the paper clip along.

UNDERSTANDING GOD:

Sometimes life gets confusing, and it looks like a maze to us. It appears to us that we may never get out of certain problems! If we were like that paper clip without the magnet, we surely would be stuck. But God is very strong and powerful and able to move us along—without us even seeing him! He has all the spiritual magnetic pull to lead us through all the problems in life. And, as Proverbs 3:5-6 says, if we acknowledge his presence in most everything we do, he will make our paths straight!

EXPERIMENT #3

CAN A MAGNET RESCUE A DROWNING PAPER CLIP?

RELATED SCRIPTURE:

Matthew 14:29-31 ...and when Peter was come down out of the ship, he walked on the water to go to Jesus. But when he saw the wind boisterous, he was afraid; and beginning to sink, he cried, saying Lord, save me. And immediately Jesus stretched forth his hand and caught him, and said unto him "O thou of little faith, wherefore didst thou doubt".

MATERIALS:

- Glass
- Tap water
- Paper clip
- One-inch horseshoe magnet

STEPS:

1. Fill the glass with tap water
2. Drop the paper clip in
3. Hold up the glass
4. Set the magnet up under the glass, beneath the paper clip
5. Slowly move the magnet to the edge of the bottom of the glass and then up the side

What happens to the paper clip? Can it be saved from the water?

ANSWER:

The paper clip should follow the magnet.

EXPLANATION:

This experiment shows that magnetism can pull through water. Water is almost completely non-magnetic, meaning that we cannot magnetize it. Glass also has no effect on a magnetic field, so the combination of glass and water should not affect the pull the magnet has on the paper clip.

UNDERSTANDING GOD:

In Matthew 14, we find the story of the Apostle Peter suddenly starting to drown after he walked on water to Jesus. However, he was spiritually "magnetized" by knowing Christ. We often get in hot water in our lives, finding ourselves so deep in a problem that we don't know how to get out. But just like Jesus saved Peter from the stormy sea, God can save us from drowning in our sorrows by lifting us up out of our woes. God doesn't solve every problem right away, but he will keep us afloat until the storms pass - if we stay "magnetized" to his loving hands!

EXPERIMENT #4

CREATING AN ELECTROMAGNET

RELATED SCRIPTURE:

Matthew 24:27 For as lightning that comes from the east is visible even in the west, so will be the coming of the Son of Man.

MATERIALS:

- One Size D Battery
- Four feet of copper wire
- Rubber band
- One large nail, like a roofing nail
- Five paper clips

STEPS:

1. Hold the nail up to the paper clips

Does the nail serve as a magnet to attract the paper clips?

2. Pinch your fingers on the copper wire about 2 ½ inches away from one end

3. Wrap the bit of wire around the nail as many times as you can, leaving about half an inch of wire free at the end

4. Wrap the rubber band around the battery so that it covers the positive end on top and the negative end underneath.

5. Lift the rubber band and lay one end of the wire under the positive end of the battery and one end of the wire under the negative end of the battery

6. Now try to lift the paper clips with the nail

What happens?

ANSWER:

The first time you held the nail to the paper clips, it would not be able to attract them and nothing would have happened. Once the nail is hooked to the battery with the cooper wire, it should have attracted the paper clips.

EXPLANATION:

Copper wire is an electric conductor, meaning it allows electricity to travel along it easily. By hooking the nail to the wire and running the wire to the battery, you are creating a magnetic field using electricity, or an electromagnetic field. The field, however, only exists when the electricity is flowing. Thus, when you disconnect the battery from the nail, it ceases to be magnetic. This works because a battery produces electrons. They collect down near the negative end of the battery. However, they will flow to the positive end if you connect them. Whatever is in between (in this case the nail) receives the electrical charge that makes it temporarily magnetic.

UNDERSTANDING GOD:

The temporary state of electro-magnetization can resemble our world at points in history. There have always been times where the spirit of God was more present and active than during others, and people have called them "magnetic times." One time was when God created the flood described in Genesis, and all of the earth went under water at his command. Another time was when the Hebrews fled Egypt under the command of Moses. Of course we're all fond of the time when Jesus lived on earth, but it has been nearly 2,000 years since that time! Many Christians are so anxious to see him again that they remember Matthew 24:27 every time there's a thunderstorm: *For as lightning that comes from the east is visible even in the west, so will be the coming of the Son of Man.* Some of these enthusiastic lovers of Christ will rush to the window during a thunderstorm to see if it's flashing from east to west—thinking that day may come soon!

Today, our world appears to be a very dull spiritual time in history; *not* very magnetic at all. Many don't believe in God, and may even try to draw Jesus' followers to their way of thinking. Like that nail that becomes a magnet, this world will someday light up and have great spiritual power while Jesus sits in the midst of us. He will draw all of us into him, just like those paper clips, and we can rejoice to be so near to him again!

EXPERIMENT #5

SHOWING HOW OPPOSITES ATTRACT IN MAGNETS

RELATED SCRIPTURE:

1 Peter 4:10 As each one has received a special gift, employ it in serving one another, as good stewards of the manifold grace of God

MATERIALS:

- Bowl
- Tap water
- Two needles
- One-inch horseshoe magnet
- Two small pieces of paper

STEPS:

1. First you need to create two magnets out of needles. With each needle, complete the following steps:

    a) Pinch the sewing needle between your thumb and finger at the halfway point

    b) Take the magnet and, using one end of the horseshoe only, rub the needle from your finger out to the point

    c) Stroke the needle 50 times this way with the magnet, always going in the same direction, always using the same end of the magnet

    d) Turn the needle and the magnet around

    e) Using the other end of the horseshoe only, rub the needle from your finger out to the eye

    f) Stroke the needle 50 times this way with the magnet, always going in the same direction, always using the same end of the magnet

2. Fill your bowl with tap water.
3. Put the pieces of paper in the water.
4. Put one needle on each piece of paper, side by side, with the points going in the same direction.

How do the needles behave?

5. Turn one needle around so that one point is pointing in the same direction as one eye.

How do the needles behave now?

ANSWERS:

When the points of the needles are facing the same direction, the points should float away from each other. When one eye and one point are facing in the same direction, the needles should float toward each other.

EXPLANATION:

Magnets always have two poles—a north pole and a south pole. Opposites always attract in magnetic force. So if two north poles or two south poles are put together, they will try to push away from each other or "repel". But if a north pole and a south pole are put together, they will attract each other and try to draw closer together.

When holding two magnets in your hands, if the magnetic pull is strong enough, you can tell when you're putting two north or two south ends together, as you will feel resistance. It will seem that the magnets are trying to get away from each other. When you put a north pole up to a south pole, they will stick to each other.

UNDERSTANDING GOD:

Opposites attract in the world of magnetism, but also in the world of school. God made us all different, and school classes are made up of lots of different types of kids. Some students will seem to be the opposite of you. Some will be talkative and friendly. Others are more serious thinkers and don't talk much. But when they do it's often something really smart! It helps to love one another when we understand that those not like us have also been given special gifts from God—just not our gifts. And we'll often find that opposites attract. If we're very talkative, we might appreciate a quiet friend more than we realize. If your "magnetic pull" seems to attract your opposite, don't try to repel that person away; God made you both special!

Five Experiments Using Gravity

Did you know that the earth is actually a giant magnet? It has a magnetic core as do the sun, moon, and planets; however, some have greater magnetic pull than others. The sun's magnetism is what keeps the earth in orbit. The earth's magnetism keeps the moon in orbit.

Gravity is the reason we don't float off into space. Everything on earth pulls toward its core due to its magnetism and constant spinning.

You've heard the expression, "Stay grounded." It means don't make bad choices or do dumb things. In church we talk about "staying grounded in God's word." That means we let our actions follow what the Bible says. Like gravity keeps our feet on the ground, God's word keeps us from floating off his paths. Let's try some experiments to see what God and gravity have in common.

EXPERIMENT #1

GRAVITY DOESN'T CARE ABOUT WEIGHT

RELATED SCRIPTURE:

Galatians 3:28 There is neither Jew nor Greek, slave nor free, male nor female, for you are all one in Christ Jesus.

MATERIALS:

- Raw potato
- Pencil
- Chair

STEPS:

1. Stand on the chair
2. Grip the potato between two fingers on one hand
3. Grip the pencil between two fingers on the other hand
4. Put your wrists together so neither object is higher than the other
5. Let go of both objects
6. Repeat a few times

Which item consistently hits the ground first?

ANSWER:

Neither. Both should hit the ground at the same time, even though the potato is much heavier.

EXPLANATION:

One would think the potato would hit the ground first because it weighs more. However, the same would hold true if you dropped a piano out a window right beside a pencil. Both would hit the ground at the same time.

One important principle of gravity is that it pulls all items toward the center of the earth with equal force. As defined by Galileo, this is called The Equivalence Principle. Weight is not an issue in free-falling objects. The speed of any free-falling object on planet earth is about 32 feet per second.

UNDERSTANDING GOD:

The Equivalence Principle is also well demonstrated in salvation. God loves us all the same, and is willing to have a relationship with fat people, skinny people, tall people, short people, loud people, shy people, old people, and young people. He draws us to him, and he doesn't care how different we are from one another. As stated in Galatians 3:28, we are all one in Christ!

EXPERIMENT #2

FINDING THE CENTER OF GRAVITY TO CREATE BALANCE

RELATED SCRIPTURE:

Romans 12:19 Dearly beloved, avenge not yourselves, but rather give place unto wrath: for it is written, Vengeance is mine; I will repay, saith the Lord.

MATERIALS:

- A 12-inch ruler without additional length at either end
- Two pennies

STEPS:

1. Put your finger under the ruler in about the center
2. Move the ruler slightly to the left or right until it balances perfectly on your finger

At which marking on the ruler is my finger? Is it closer to four inches, six inches, or eight inches?

3. Between the 11- and 12-inch markings, place a penny.

What happens to the ruler now?

4. Balance the ruler again, and have someone else put a penny between the 11- and 12-inch markings and another one between the 1- and 2-inch markings.

What happens to the ruler this time?

ANSWERS:

The first time, the ruler should have balanced at six inches. When you added the first penny, the ruler became imbalanced and either toppled or you had to catch it. The second time, adding both pennies, the ruler should have balanced at six inches again.

EXPLANATION:

Here we need to look at a concept called the "center of gravity." If an object is equally weighted, meaning all parts of it weigh about the same, the center of gravity will be in the middle. Hence, in a perfect 12-inch ruler, the center will be at the halfway point, or at the six-inch point.

When you add weight to one side or the other, you change an object's center of gravity. If you add equal weight to both sides, the center of gravity will return to the center of the item.

UNDERSTANDING GOD:

Often in Scripture, balances are weighed by scales, and scales are a symbol of justice. We have a very just God who considers our pains and hurts when others are mean to us, and he is more than capable of "balancing out" the score. This is why it's important not to seek revenge when somebody is mean or hit somebody back if they hit you first. Always remember Romans 12:19: "Dearly beloved, avenge not yourselves, but rather give place unto wrath: for it is written, Vengeance is mine; I will repay, saith the Lord."

When somebody comes along who adds weight to our load and makes us feel like we're going to topple, let God handle it. He'll give us whatever we need to stay balanced, no matter what unjust things life throws at us.

Experiment #3

Changing the Center of Gravity Keeps the Disciple Standing

Related Scripture:

Psalm 27:1 The LORD is my light and my salvation--whom shall I fear? The LORD is the stronghold of my life--of whom shall I be afraid?

Materials:

- Empty toilet-paper roll
- Small plastic Easter egg (the colored kind that opens so that you can stick candy in it)
- Scotch tape
- Can of play dough, any color
- Marker pen

Steps:

1. Unscrew the plastic Easter egg. Keep the round bottom, and put the taller top off to the side.
2. Lay out one six-inch strip of Scotch tape, sticky side up.
3. Stick the very bottom point of the egg onto the center of the tape and press down so it sticks (sides facing up).
4. Place one end of the toilet-paper roll on top of the egg, *but not so that it completely swallows the egg and rests on the table.* Think of the tube as a little man and the egg as its feet. You want the egg to stick out from the bottom as much as it can.
5. Have someone else roll the tape upwards onto either side of the tube so that the tube is now taped to the egg bottom.
6. Secure with a second piece of tape.
7. Draw a face on the top of the toilet-paper roll so that it looks like a little disciple.
8. Stand the tube up straight so that the little disciple is balancing on the egg bottom.
9. Let go.

What happens to the disciple?

10. Roll a wad of play dough into a ball that is about two inches across.

11. Drop the play-dough ball into the tube so that it rests in the egg bottom.

12. Stand the tube up straight again.

13. Let go.

What happens this time?

14. Try to push the little disciple over.

Does he stay down?

ANSWERS:

The first time you let go of the tube, it was empty. The force of gravity pulled it down.

The second time, you had dropped a weight into the bottom. The result was that it would not fall down, and when pushed over, it would pop back up.

EXPLANATION:

While he was empty, the top of the little disciple weighed just about as much as the bottom. That means his "center of gravity" was at his "geometric center," or just about around his belly. Therefore, gravity pulled at his center, and he toppled over sideways.

By adding the heavier play-dough ball, we changed the little disciple's center of gravity to the bottom. His heaviest point was no longer at his geometric center halfway up. Therefore, gravity pulled at the bottom. As the top is lighter, it is able to remain standing.

UNDERSTANDING GOD:

We've all heard Christians say things like, "It was a terrible ordeal, but God kept me standing throughout." God doesn't let us fall when we walk with him in our journey through life. Things can make us "stumble," feel pain and disappointment, or even behave badly for a while. But God is like the heavy ball. He gets us back to our feet with his strength, defying all things that say we should stay down!

Experiment #4

How Heat Affects Gravity

Related Scripture:

1 Thessalonians 5:16-18: Rejoice always; pray without ceasing; in everything give thanks, for this is God's will for you in Christ Jesus.

Materials:

- Two hot pancakes, the same size
- One container of cold syrup from the refrigerator
- One container of hot syrup from the microwave
- Two tablespoons
- Two plates

Steps:

1. If you're starting with room temperature syrup, you can put one-fourth cup in the freezer for 15 minutes and one-fourth cup in the microwave for 20 seconds.
2. Put two hot pancakes on two different plates
3. Pour a few tablespoons of hot syrup into the center of one pancake
4. Time how long the hot syrup takes to get to the edge of the pancake.
5. Pour a few tablespoons of cold syrup into the center of the other pancake.
6. Time how long the cold syrup takes to get to the edge of the pancake

Which syrup got to the edge of the pancake first?

Answer:

The hot syrup was easier for the force of gravity to contend with, and it should have reached the edges of the pancake first.

EXPLANATION:

Gravity is partly responsible for the fact that liquids don't take shape easily. As the weight of most liquid is evenly distributed throughout, gravity pulls it downward all at once. However, hot items will respond to the force of gravity more quickly than cold items. This has to do with "viscosity," which is the rate at which a liquid can move. The thicker the liquid, the higher its viscosity, and the more resistant it is to gravity. Hence, the cold syrup takes longer to respond to gravitational pull than hot liquid, which moves quickly.

UNDERSTANDING GOD:

God wants us to be "on fire" for him! In other words, he wants us to be hot—like hot syrup that moves fast and far. The most on-fire Christians tend to be the ones who follow 1 Thessalonians 5:16-18. This verse tells us to rejoice always (even in bad circumstances, because God loves a positive attitude). It tells us to pray without ceasing (or in other words, make God such a part of your life that he seems to be present in everything). It tells us to be thankful in all circumstances (because bad times make us stronger and more appreciative when the good times come back!). If we try to do these things, we will find that we are hot and on fire for God—and we'll move fast, and reach our goals more quickly!

Experiment #5

Putting a Spin on Gravity

Related Scripture:

John 6:40 For my Father's will is that everyone who looks to the Son and believes in Him shall have eternal life, and I will raise Him up at the last day."

Materials:

- Clear glass
- Small ball such as a ping-pong ball

Steps:

1. Put the ball on a table
2. Cover the ball with the glass
3. Using swift, circular motions in your wrist, vibrate the glass in little circles until the ball begins to spin inside its edge
4. Continuing to spin the little circles, lift the glass
5. Stop spinning

What happened to the ball when I lifted the glass? What happened to the ball when I stopped spinning?

Answer:

When you lifted the glass, if you were spinning fast enough, the ball would rise with the glass and continue to spin around its edge. When you stopped spinning, it slowed and dropped out.

Explanation:

We have seen one of many exceptions to the law of gravity, which occurs when we pit energy against gravity. Any object in motion is said to have kinetic energy. The faster the object moves the more kinetic energy it contains. The more kinetic energy an object contains, the less it is subject to gravity. As an object slows, the kinetic energy dissipates, and the object becomes subject to gravity once again.

UNDERSTANDING GOD:

God created the laws of this earth, but he has higher laws that can break the laws of earth. Just like the force of gravity can be broken, the power of death can be broken. We don't have to "fall down" in death and cease to exist, even though it would appear that's what we do. God's laws are miraculous, as the spinning ball appears miraculous. When we die, we don't stay down; we go to heaven to be with our Lord! Jesus put the ultimate spin on death when he rose on the third day after his crucifixion!

Made in the USA
Middletown, DE
26 September 2017